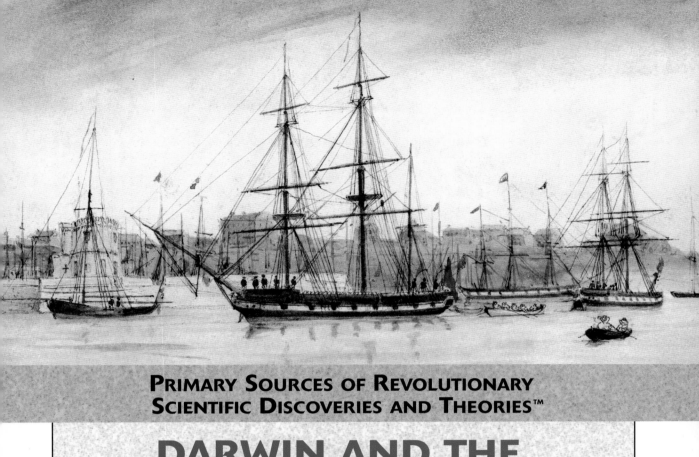

PRIMARY SOURCES OF REVOLUTIONARY SCIENTIFIC DISCOVERIES AND THEORIES™

DARWIN AND THE THEORY OF EVOLUTION

ROBERT GREENBERGER

rosen central
Primary Source™

The Rosen Publishing Group, Inc., New York

To Robbie, my evolutionary supporter

Published in 2005 by The Rosen Publishing Group, Inc.
29 East 21st Street, New York, NY 10010

First Edition

Library of Congress Cataloging-in-Publication Data

Greenberger, Robert.
Darwin and the theory of evolution / by Robert Greenberger.
   p. cm. — (Primary sources of revolutionary scientific discoveries and theories)
Includes bibliographical references and index.
ISBN 1-4042-0306-0 (lib. bdg.)
1. Darwin, Charles, 1809–1882. 2. Naturalists—England—Biography. 3. Evolution
(Biology)—History.
I. Title. II. Series.
QH31.D2G7199 2004
576.8'2—dc22
                                                                          2004006782

Printed in Hong Kong

On the front cover: Painting of Joseph Hooker, Charles Lyell, and Charles Darwin

On the back cover (*top to bottom*): Nicolaus Copernicus, Charles Darwin, Edwin Hubble, Johannes Kepler, Gregor Mendel, Dmitry Mendeleyev, Isaac Newton, James Watson *(right)* and Francis Crick *(left)*

CONTENTS

INTRODUCTION How Did We Get Here? 4

CHAPTER 1 Youth of a Naturalist 6

CHAPTER 2 Darwin's World 11

CHAPTER 3 The *Beagle* Sets Sail 16

CHAPTER 4 The Road to Discovery 24

CHAPTER 5 Evolution of the Species 37

CHAPTER 6 The Evolution of Darwinism 45

TIMELINE 52

PRIMARY SOURCE TRANSCRIPTIONS 54

GLOSSARY 56

FOR MORE INFORMATION 58

FOR FURTHER READING 59

BIBLIOGRAPHY 60

PRIMARY SOURCE IMAGE LIST 61

INDEX 62

INTRODUCTION

As much as man has looked up at the sky and wondered what is out there among the stars, he has also looked at the world in which he lives, and asked, "How did I get here?" Man looked for ways to explain things that seemed unexplainable. Different populations around the world believed in a variety of gods, which helped explain how the universe was created and how it worked. Each people's mythology had its own explanation for how the world was formed and why.

HOW DID WE GET HERE?

As time went on and technology advanced, societies grew more efficient in the way in which they fed and sheltered themselves. This efficiency gave man the time to ponder questions about where he came from.

Yet, as man learned more about the world through observation and scientific study, it became apparent that the myths believed by people of the past did not always support the evidence that the scientists discovered. By the nineteenth century, an entire branch of science grew around the idea that mankind evolved, or gradually changed, in response to its environment. Many scientists believed that all living creatures, including man, evolved. It wasn't until Charles Darwin's voyage on the ship HMS *Beagle*, however, that this theory was tested.

One of the instruments Darwin used to navigate during his five-year voyage on the HMS *Beagle* was the sextant shown here. Common during Darwin's time, the sextant is an instrument used for measuring latitude and longitude. It does this by measuring distances on Earth, from which it calculates the distances to celestial bodies such as the planets and stars. By knowing the positions of the stars, the user of the sextant can know his or her exact place on Earth. The sextant was critical for Darwin and his crew to navigate during their voyage. The navigational tools in the nineteenth century were primitive compared to today's radar and satellite mapping technologies, which makes Darwin's voyage all the more impressive.

Darwin was born at a time when scientific achievement was valued, and the fruits of scientific labors were rewarded at every level of society. With a zest for learning, Darwin painstakingly studied a variety of plant and animal species to see how they survived in the world. The result of his research was a revolutionary idea—the origin of life. The ideas that Darwin developed and the things he discovered on that voyage helped change the way we view our place in the world.

CHAPTER 1

Charles Robert Darwin was born to Susannah and Robert Darwin, on February 12, 1809, at his family's home, called the Mount, in Shrewsbury, England, in Shropshire County. Young Bobby, as Charles was called, came from a distinguished family. His grandfathers were Erasmus Darwin, a poet and scientist, and Josiah Wedgwood, founder of Wedgwood pottery. Life in early nineteenth-century England was fairly quiet for Charles, that is, until his mother died when he was just eight years old.

YOUTH OF A NATURALIST

Charles and his older brother, named Erasmus after his grandfather, attended Reverend Samuel Butler's school. Charles showed a great interest in learning. But rather than studying Greek and Latin like most students of the time, he was taken with the English poetry of William Wordsworth and Lord Byron.

When Charles was a teenager, science began to captivate him, so much so, in fact, that he and Erasmus built a chemistry lab in a garden shed. Charles enjoyed chemistry. His friends later nicknamed him Gas.

Doctor Darwin

Charles's father, Robert, was a physician. He took Charles out of his current school in 1825—Robert felt that it was a waste of

In this 1840 portrait by George Richmond, Darwin is still a young man. Though he is shown as being only in his early thirties, he had accomplished more by this time than most people achieve in a lifetime. He had graduated from Christ's College in Cambridge in 1831 and boarded the HMS *Beagle* that same year. During his historic five-year voyage on the *Beagle*, Darwin conducted research that would revolutionize the way scientists studied man's origins two decades later with the publication of *On the Origin of Species*. The book was so revolutionary that the theories it explained would be debated throughout the next 150 years.

time. He thought that his son had no direction in life. He did not realize that Charles had developed an interest in science, particularly animal life. He decided that Charles was to become a doctor, so he sent his son to join Erasmus at the University of Edinburgh in Scotland.

Charles was not a good medical student. He disliked the sight of blood and found the work tedious. He did, though, like studying the art of taxidermy, which he learned from a former African slave named John Edmonstone.

During his second year in Scotland, Darwin joined the Plinian Society, a club for naturalists. He was taken with their intellectual debates, which exposed him to ideas of how man was created not by God, but by gradual changes in form over time. These ideas were different from the Judeo-Christian teachings of the creation of the universe on which he was raised.

Evolutionary Ideas

While at the university, Darwin met Robert Grant, a zoologist. The two became close friends. At this time, Darwin began collecting fossils and learning more about animal life. Grant has been credited with being the first person to interest Darwin in the theory of evolution. Evolution is the belief that organisms change over time—they adapt to and survive in their environments. Darwin's interest was further fueled by the writings of French zoologist Jean-Baptiste Lamarck.

After two years, Darwin, quite sick of the sight of blood, quit medical school and went to London. He joined his uncle Josiah Wedgwood II for a trip to Paris. As he vacationed, Robert Darwin, still fretting over his son dropping out of medical school and becoming an idle gentleman, made plans for Charles to study for the clergy. He enrolled him at Christ's College at Cambridge University.

During the summer, before school began, Charles fell in love with Fanny Owen, the sister of one of his best friends. They spent many hours together, talking, riding horses, and playing cards. Charles also spent that fall preparing for Cambridge, completing required studies. He began classes at the end of 1827.

But rather than study the Bible, Charles developed a fondness for collecting beetles. This led to a further interest in the field of naturalism. He attended lectures on botany given by the Reverend John Stevens Henslow. Darwin saw this as a possible career path, and he pursued his studies with enthusiasm.

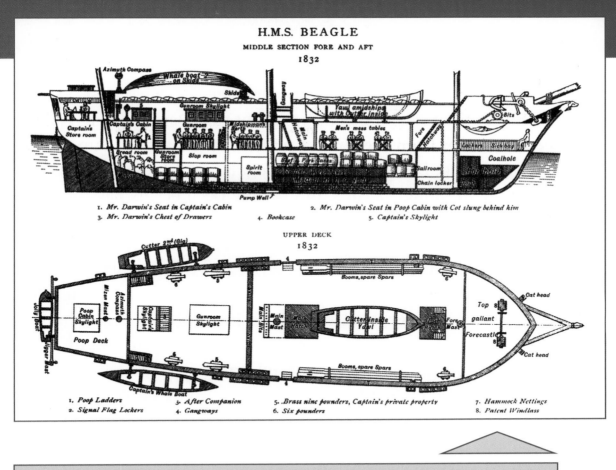

H.M.S. BEAGLE
MIDDLE SECTION FORE AND AFT
1832

1. Mr. Darwin's Seat in Captain's Cabin   2. Mr. Darwin's Seat in Poop Cabin with Cot slung behind him
3. Mr. Darwin's Chest of Drawers   4. Bookcase   5. Captain's Skylight

UPPER DECK
1832

1. Poop Ladders   3. After Companion   5. Brass nine pounders, Captain's private property   7. Hammock Nettings
2. Signal Flag Lockers   4. Gangways   6. Six pounders   8. Patent Windlass

This 1832 illustration shows the deck plans of the HMS *Beagle*. The top schematic offers a side, cross-section view of the ship with its various decks and compartments. This view shows us that even though the *Beagle* was of decent size, space remained tight. Supplies and equipment for the long journey left little room to relax for those on board. The bottom view shows the floor plan for the upper deck. With little room down below, the upper deck was probably where Darwin spent a lot of his time. This is also where he would have been able to observe the natural environment on the journey for his studies.

Boarding the *Beagle*

By 1829, it was clear that Darwin was not interested in joining the clergy. Darwin spent his spring break with the Reverend Frederick Hope, a noted entomologist. They spent many hours together. The reverend provided more samples for Charles's growing beetle collection.

Within the year, it became apparent that Darwin preferred his study of beetles to his romance with Fanny. They broke up the following spring. Darwin became a regular at Professor Henslow's Friday night dinner parties, and botany became his passion.

Despite his general lack of interest in the course work, Darwin passed his final exams in January 1831, placing tenth in his class. Finished with school, Darwin was ready to become a countryside clergyman while indulging in his scientific interests in his personal time. Henslow, though, suggested to Darwin that he travel first, words that would prove fateful.

That spring, Darwin prepared for a trip to the Canary Islands, off the coast of Spain, while attending geology lectures by Professor Adam Sedgwick. Geology had bored Darwin in the past, but Sedgwick brought the topic to life and fully engaged Darwin's attention.

Rather than go alone, Darwin asked his friend Marmaduke Ramsay to accompany him on the journey. In the final weeks before departure, Sedgwick lectured about geology so Darwin would know what he was observing on the islands. But Darwin's plans came to a crashing halt—Ramsay died suddenly. Darwin was stricken with grief and could not travel to the islands. Then Professor Henslow and the Reverend George Peacock wrote to Darwin and told him of an opening on a ship—the HMS *Beagle*, bound for South America. Suddenly, things began to turn around.

CHAPTER 2

DARWIN'S WORLD

Although the nineteenth century may not seem like that long ago, changes in the world since then have been dramatic. At the beginning of the nineteenth century, Europe was engaged in the Napoleonic Wars. The United States was just a young and upcoming country. Scientists were just beginning to understand the nature of electricity and magnetism. The Industrial Revolution, a period of great technological advancement, was transforming society. Much of the world's population was poorly educated. Many people turned to religion, which offered an explanation as to how the universe was created. Many people believed then, as they do today, that God created the universe and all the creatures on Earth. Today, this belief is known as creationism. During the nineteenth century, however, anyone who did not believe in creationism was considered a heretic, someone who opposes the beliefs of the Judeo-Christian Church.

However, many scientists of the time were beginning to wonder if creationism was true. If so, then why did some creatures live only in certain parts of the world? Why did some creatures, such as the dinosaurs, become extinct? During the nineteenth century, the first explorations of dinosaur fossils began, causing people to wonder how these creatures once ruled the world only to vanish, while other similar species flourished.

During the early nineteenth century, the Industrial Revolution was taking place, as shown in this 1834 painting by Alfred Rethel titled *The Harkort Factory at Burg Wetter*. Great advances in industry were under way. What came with the Industrial Revolution were great discoveries in science, too. Scientists were beginning to question whether we could depend on religion any longer to answer the mysteries of the universe. As this painting shows, Darwin's world was one of great change and ambition.

Evolution Before Darwin

The theory of evolution began long ago. The ancient Greek philosophers pondered the issue of evolution, as seen in ancient texts that have survived the ages. Then various scientists and theorists touched on the subject of evolution, but they were usually lone voices. These thinkers were largely ignored by their peers and the people of the time. Oftentimes, people did not want to hear what the scientists had to say because they feared the wrath of religious authorities who would not stand for anything that differed from the religion's belief of how the world was created.

Many, however, acknowledged that there had to be some evolutionary connection. For example, in 1764, the French philosopher and scientist Charles Bonnet created a linear chart showing those evolutionary connections, with man at the top and mold at the bottom.

Carolus Linnaeus

Carolus Linnaeus (1707–1778), Swedish botanist and explorer, developed a classification system that grouped animals into categories such as *Canidae* (dogs) and *Felidae* (cats). From here, he developed theories of hybridization, showing how different species mated and produced creatures of mixed species. Linnaeus's theory of hybridization suggested that species could change over time, supporting the idea that they evolve.

Georges Buffon

Linnaeus's ideas resembled those of French naturalist Georges Buffon (1707–1788). Buffon's theory of degeneration states that by looking at a species today, its lineage can be traced back to an ancestral starting point. This ancestral starting point was one species from which all others evolved. For example, an ancient feline, or cat, species developed into present-day lions, tigers, pumas, and house cats.

Erasmus Darwin

Charles Darwin's own grandfather, Erasmus Darwin (1731–1802), combined the theories of creationism and evolution. In his book *Zoonomia* (1796), he put forth the notion that God designed life, but also designed it to be self-improving. He said that animals were meant to grow and adapt to their changing surroundings. Erasmus so impressed and impacted Charles's thinking, that in his later years, Charles wrote a biography about his grandfather.

The early 1800s was also a thrilling time of discovery in a wide variety of scientific fields. Many scientists toured and lectured before public audiences. Charles was exposed to many of these naturalists throughout his developing years.

An Unknown World

During this time of discovery, the HMS *Beagle* was being prepared as one of several ships scheduled to map South America. Robert Fitzroy, captain of the *Beagle*, recognized that the long voyage would require that a variety of men be aboard for companionship. He desired a scholar-gentleman who could help describe the areas that were being charted, as well as relieve the tedium between ports of call. When the opening presented itself, Darwin took his spot on the *Beagle*.

Charles's father, Robert, would never consider such a thing and refused to give his adult son permission. Robert continued to believe Charles's interest in science was merely a passing

ZOONOMIA;

OR,

THE LAWS OF ORGANIC LIFE.

PART II.

CONTAINING

A CATALOGUE OF DISEASES

DISTRIBUTED INTO

NATURAL CLASSES ACCORDING TO THEIR PROXIMATE CAUSES,

WITH THEIR

SUBSEQUENT ORDERS, GENERA, AND SPECIES,

AND WITH

THEIR METHODS OF CURE.

Hæc, ut potero, explicabo; nec tamen, quasi Pythius Apollo, certa ut sint et fixa, quæ dixero; sed ut Homunculus unus e multis probabiliora conjecturâ sequens.
Cic. Tusc. Disp. l. i. 9.

A 2

PREFACE.

ALL diseases originate in the exuberance, deficiency, or retrograde action, of the faculties of the sensorium, as their proximate cause; and consist in the disordered motions of the fibres of the body, as the proximate effect of the exertions of those disordered faculties.

The sensorium possesses four distinct powers, or faculties, which are occasionally exerted, and produce all the motions of the fibrous parts of the body; these are the faculties of producing fibrous motions in consequence of irritation which is excited by external bodies; in consequence of sensation which is excited by pleasure or pain; in consequence of volition which is excited by desire or aversion; and in consequence of association which is excited by other fibrous motions. We are hence supplied with four natural classes of diseases derived from their proximate causes; which we shall term those of irritation, those of sensation, those of volition, and those of association.

In the subsequent classification of diseases I have not adhered to the methods of any of those, who have preceded me; the principal of whom are the great names of Sauvages and Cullen; but have nevertheless availed myself, as much as I could, of their definitions and distinctions.

The essential characteristic of a disease consists in its proximate cause, as is well observed by Doctor Cullen, in his Nosologia Methodica, T. ii. Prolegom.
p. xxix.

Charles was not the only Darwin who was a naturalist and author. Charles's grandfather Erasmus Darwin had his own theories about evolution, which he expressed in his book *Zoonomia; or, The Laws of Organic Life*, shown here. Erasmus didn't separate the theories of creationism and evolution like Charles would later do. Instead, Erasmus combined the theories of creationism and evolution and proposed that they were both valid in explaining the origins of man. He wrote that though species evolve, they were created by God to do so. In this way, they were creatures of God but ones that were designed to be self-improving. (See page 54 for an excerpt.)

fad and that the young man remained adrift. Charles's uncle Josiah, though, stepped in and won permission for Charles to join the excursion.

Charles then hastened to London to meet with Fitzroy, hoping the offer remained. Plans to depart in September were gradually moved back until the ship finally set sail on Tuesday, December 27, 1831.

CHAPTER 3

**THE
BEAGLE
SETS SAIL**

In early December 1831, Darwin boarded the HMS *Beagle* for the first time a few weeks before it set sail. He prepared his small cabin located above the captain's quarters. The space was nine feet (2.7 meters) wide by eleven feet (3.25 m) long and only five feet (1.5 m) high. Part of the cabin was taken up with one of the masts rising through it.

Darwin boarded early because he wanted to adjust to shipboard life prior to departure. When the ship finally left dock a few weeks later, Darwin was almost immediately sea sick, a condition that never truly left him over the next five years.

The *Beagle* finally set sail at around eleven in the morning. The first port of call was Santa Cruz, Tenerife Island, in the Canary Islands. But rather than wait for a routine quarantine period, Fitzroy insisted that they sail on.

The *Beagle* Docks

Darwin finally set foot on foreign soil on January 16, 1832. The crew stopped at the Cape Verde Islands, off the western coast of Africa. Almost immediately, Darwin made a discovery that combined his various interests in geology and naturalism. He found a band of fossil shells forty-five feet (13.7 m) above sea level. This made him question how the fossils rose so high.

This watercolor painting offers a rare glimpse of the expedition of the HMS *Beagle*. The painting was done by artist Conrad Martens, who was onboard the ship with Darwin and his crew during the five-year voyage. In the background is Mount Sarmiento in the Tierra del Fuego Archipelago at the southern tip of South America. The ship arrived at this point just before reaching the Galápagos Islands. To the left of the mountains is the HMS *Beagle* in port.

The *Beagle* remained in port for twenty-three days. It then set out for Brazil, arriving in the port city of Salvador at the end of February 1832. Darwin took solitary walks, marveling at the rich foliage and exotic animal life. The *Beagle* remained in Brazil through the spring of that year. The ship traveled along the coast, stopping in many ports of call. At each stop, Darwin continued to take long hikes and collect countless specimens.

In August, Darwin sent a load of specimens, along with detailed notes describing them, back to Henslow in Cambridge

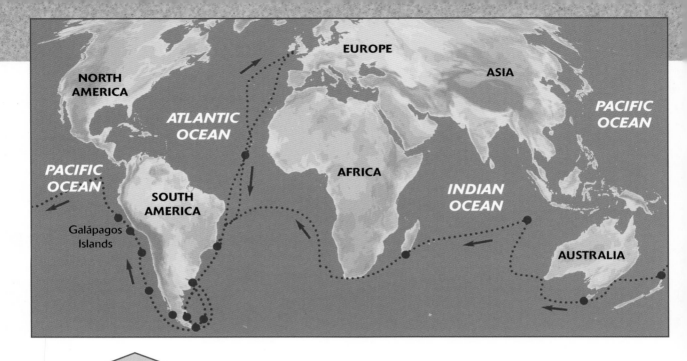

Darwin's voyage on the HMS *Beagle* brought him around the world over a period of five years. As this map shows, his ports allowed him to study the environments of several continents. Starting from Europe, the *Beagle* reached its first port in January 1832, the Cape Verde Islands off the west coast of Africa. From there, it was to the east coast of South America. South America was, by far, the richest study for Darwin. It was here that he studied the species and environment of the Galápagos Islands in September 1835, where he gathered most of his materials and specimens to formulate his theory of evolution. The HMS *Beagle* then found its way to Australia and New Zealand in early 1836, making its way back to Falmouth, England, on October 2 of that year.

for safekeeping. By then, Darwin had earned the nicknames "Flycatcher" and "Philosopher" from the ship's crew because of his large collection of specimens. Fitzroy called the growing collection junk, but each item was precious to Darwin.

Next, the ship sailed to Patagonia, a large region in southern South America that is now part of Argentina. There, Darwin collected fossils, bits of bone, and feathers, among other things he had never before encountered. He struggled to accurately record their features in the hopes that more experienced naturalists could later help to identify them.

Darwin kept detailed notes on his voyage around the world. Shown here are two manuscript pages of what would be published as *The Journal of a Voyage in HMS Beagle*, known now as simply *The Voyage of the Beagle*. The journal explains the day-by-day account of Darwin's observations and discoveries. Though Darwin's *On the Origin of Species* is considered his most important work, *The Voyage of the Beagle* shows how Darwin formulated his ideas for the theory of evolution. (See page 54 for an excerpt.)

Darwin sent a second shipment to Henslow in November before the ship headed for Tierra del Fuego, on the southern tip of South America. There, Darwin first encountered native peoples, those who still lived in the jungle and were considered to be savages by the Europeans.

The Falklands

By March 1833, the crew of the *Beagle* began mapping the Falkland Islands, which the British had claimed from Argentina just months earlier. Fascinated by bird and animal fossils found there, Darwin spent his time comparing those specimens with everything he had collected to date.

In May of that year, Darwin remained in Maldonado, Uruguay, while the ship headed back to Montevideo. He took a twelve-day journey into the interior, using hired gauchos, or cowboys, for help. Recognizing the need for full-time help, Darwin wrote home, asking his father to provide money so he could hire a servant. When permission arrived, Darwin asked the ship's odd-job man, Syms Covington, to take the role.

After sending a third shipment of specimens to Henslow in July 1833, Darwin was ready to see new locales. Darwin later learned that Henslow had taken to reading his letters aloud to the Philosophical Society of Cambridge. This earned Darwin an early reputation there as being an excellent naturalist and observer.

In August, the *Beagle* arrived at the Rio Negro. Darwin traveled inland again, ultimately arriving at Bahia Blanca in Argentina. At one point, he found a fossil of an animal he had never seen before. The fossil was under a layer of white shells similar to the ones he first saw months earlier. He puzzled over this new discovery, wondering how these shells, which he first found forty-five feet (13.7 m) above sea level, also turned up at ground level. Also, what animal made these fossils? As the group left Montevideo in November, Darwin sent his fourth shipment to England. In Uruguay, he continued to collect fossils, consumed by this new passion.

Into the Pacific

On Darwin's twenty-fifth birthday, Captain Fitzroy named the highest mountain in the Tierra del Fuego region Mount Darwin, in Charles's honor. By April 1834, the ship had sailed around

Cape Horn at the southern tip of South America, leaving the Atlantic Ocean and entering the Pacific Ocean.

Darwin became quite ill that summer. Historians believe that this illness, the first of many noteworthy illnesses, turned him into a recluse in later years. (Based on the recorded symptoms, doctors today suspect he was infected during the voyage with Chagas's disease, a form of sleeping sickness.) He was deemed unfit to return to the ship until late October.

Finally, in November, Darwin returned to the *Beagle*. It headed for the Chonos Archipelago. Darwin found wild potatoes growing there, which amused him. He didn't expect to see potatoes growing so far away from home.

In February 1835, while studying in Valdivia, in western Chile, Darwin experienced his first earthquake. Although the quake did not do much damage to Valdivia, other surrounding areas were hit hard. As the ship and crew traveled north along the Pacific coast, they saw the devastation caused by the quake. In March, Darwin spent a few days on the island of Quiriquina and in what was left of the mainland port town of Concepción. The earthquake had leveled much of the town. While there, Darwin noted that some of the land had risen several feet as a result of the earthquake. He concluded that much of South America was rising due to such activity. This confirmed British geologist Charles Lyell's belief that land masses rose over time. This theory provided evidence for the belief that Earth was far older than previously believed.

Darwin was introduced to Lyell's work years earlier by someone who suggested he would get a laugh out of Lyell's theories. Instead, he was fascinated and here he was helping prove Lyell right. Darwin spent the spring studying the recent earthquake's effects on the land. In July, the *Beagle* arrived in Lima, Peru, to take on provisions for the next leg of the journey.

The Galápagos

On September 15, 1835, members of the crew spotted the next port of call—the Galápagos Islands, 500 miles (800 km) west of Ecuador. When Darwin first stepped foot on the Galápagos's Hood Island, the black lava covering the shoreline intrigued him. He had never seen anything like it before.

For the next couple of weeks, the ship and crew explored several islands. In October, Darwin and several others stayed on James Island for one week to continue their research. Darwin thought he collected an impressive number of specimens there, but this collection was dwarfed by what he discovered when the ship arrived in Tahiti that November. He was amazed by the variety and quantity of lush vegetation, which was unlike anything he had witnessed since leaving Europe.

Australia and New Zealand

By early 1836, the *Beagle* found its way to Australia and New Zealand. Although neither of these ports impressed Darwin as much as South America, he did take time to study the geology of both lands to compare against his notes from their other stops. For example, when they stopped at the Cocos Islands in the Indian Ocean in April, Darwin noted that the islands were almost entirely made of coral. He speculated that they must have been part of a huge coral reef that was once submerged, but was now exposed due to the lowering sea level. He compared these observations with those he made on Quiriquina Island after the earthquake. He figured that movements in the earth, such as

Darwin's microscope, shown here, was an essential tool for helping him study his collection and formulate the theories that he would publish in *On the Origin of Species*. Despite how scientifically forward-looking *Origin* was, Darwin's instruments, including this microscope, were quite primitive compared to those of today. This microscope was so unsophisticated that it had to be placed near the window so that daylight could help illuminate the objects under view. The cylindrical piece at the top of the microscope is the eyepiece, through which the observer looks. The flat, rectangular piece in the middle is a small piece of glass on which specimens are placed. Directly below that is a small mirror.

those caused by earthquakes, may have been how the shells found their position high above sea level.

By summer, the crew was ready to go home. It made its way back to Europe and arrived in Falmouth, England, on October 2. The four-year, nine-month, and five-day voyage was complete. However, Darwin's work was really just beginning.

CHAPTER 4

When Darwin arrived back home, his family was thrilled to see him alive and healthy. Almost immediately, he set about corresponding with friends and fellow scientists, making plans to analyze the materials he had gathered. Darwin encountered problems at various museums because they were flooded with fossils and other materials from the British colonies around the world. The backlog was going to present a serious challenge to Darwin in getting his findings to those collections.

At his uncle's suggestion, Darwin began organizing his records and thought about writing a book. After spending time in seclusion, cataloging his fossils, Darwin finally made a public appearance. He presented a paper to the Royal Geological Society on January 4, 1837, discussing his belief that South America rose through geologic movements over time and how the local species adapted to their new surroundings.

THE ROAD TO DISCOVERY

An Observation

Darwin continued his research through the spring, still aided by Syms Covington. Slowly, he came to the realization that the various fossils and collected specimens in his possession suggested

1. Geospiza magnirostris
3. Geospiza parvula.

2. Geospiza fortis.
4. Certhidea olivasea.

Shown here are Darwin's illustrations, published in *Voyage of the Beagle*, of the various species of finches he observed on the Galápagos Islands. The main difference between the species, Darwin noted, was the shapes of their beaks. The different islands of the Galápagos had different environments with different varieties of food. This meant that the finches had to adapt to their environments by using different feeding strategies. It was these different feeding strategies that forced each species of finch to adopt its respective style of beak. Since each of these species evolved from one single species, Darwin concluded that organisms evolve according to their different environments.

a new theory on how species grow differently from one another. The various birds that Darwin brought back were all distinct species of finches. The main difference between these birds was the shape of their beaks. Darwin wanted to understand how these distinct forms came to be. He neglected, though, to label the location where each finch was collected. He wrote to his former crewmates, hoping they could recall where certain things were gathered.

Within months, after detailed accounts from his shipmates, Darwin had enough information to conclude that each distinct version of finch was found on separate islands of the Galápagos. There were thirteen distinct species of finch spread over the dozen small islands. To Darwin, this meant that a single species of finch traveled from the mainland, several hundred miles away, to each island and adapted to the specific environments of each island. Over time, these finches evolved into their own individual species. The shapes of their beaks differed because of their different feeding strategies.

As Darwin worked on his own studies, he continued to stay abreast of other scientific developments. When he read about monkey fossils found in Africa, Darwin noted to himself the idea that humans may trace their origins to these animals because of the physical similarities between the species. However, he was learning during this time that despite the fascinating scientific discoveries being made, most scientists still held tightly to their religious beliefs of creation.

Darwin's Notebooks

By the summer of 1837, Darwin was compiling his notes into book form. Fitzroy and Darwin were collaborating on a multi-volume work titled *Narrative of the Surveying Voyages of HMS Adventure and Beagle*. Darwin's portion, called *Journal and Remarks, 1832-1836*, was to be the third volume of the set. At this time, however, Darwin was suffering from bouts of his illness. Despite this, he completed his portion of the manuscript. Captain Fitzroy, however, was late with his contribution, which

This page from Darwin's first notebook on the transmutation of species illustrates his theory of transmutation. The tree diagrams Darwin's theory of how all species, each represented by one branch of the tree, began its evolutionary timeline at a single point. In this notebook, Darwin asked himself four key questions about transmutation, adaptation, formation of species, and similarities between species. They proved to be key questions because this notebook built the foundation for theories he would express in the 1839 publication, *Narrative of the Surveying Voyages of HMS Adventure and Beagle*, and *On the Origin of Species*. (See page 54 for an excerpt.)

delayed publication until 1839. A few weeks after the multivolume set was published in 1839, Darwin's book was reissued under the title *Journal of Researches into the Geology and Natural History of the Various Countries Visited by HMS Beagle, Under the Command of Captain Fitzroy, R.N., from 1832 to 1836*. The work is most commonly referred to as the *Journal of Researches* or sometimes the *Voyage of the Beagle*.

While waiting for Fitzroy to complete his manuscript, Darwin started a new notebook in the summer of 1837, in which he posed several questions to himself:

- What evidence is there that species go through the process of transmutation?

- How do species adapt to a changing environment?
- How are new species formed?
- Why are there similarities between different species?

In his notes, Darwin began to theorize how species changed over time due to changes in their environment. This process is called transmutation. He diagrammed the way a particular species evolved over time. One of the challenges that Darwin faced was determining how animals moved from one place to another, like the finches that migrated from the mainland to the Galápagos Islands. These questions were the basis of Darwin's research through the fall and into the winter of 1838.

At the end of winter, Darwin began another notebook. Known as his C notebook, Darwin filled the pages with his theories about transmutation. By this time, Darwin had written to experts in various fields, from dog breeders to veterinarians, asking very specific questions about crossbreeding—the mating of different species or breeds to produce new forms of life. The answers he received from the experts helped him to refine his theories about how crossbreeding took place in the wild. Darwin was careful, though, not to announce his theories before they were fully developed. After all, there was no value in risking public censure until his theories could be successfully defended.

Sir John Sebright

It was becoming clear to Darwin that species adapted to their environments. Those species that changed to become more fit for their environments survived and even thrived. Other species that did not adapt died out. Darwin began to question not only why this happened, but also how this happened.

Darwin found a possible answer to these questions in Sir John Sebright's 1809 pamphlet, *The Art of Improving Breeds of Domestic Animals*. Sebright suggested that the weaker species do not live long enough to pass on their traits to the next generation. Darwin thought about these ideas with regard to his finches. It occurred to him that the finches would have multiplied to the point where the resources on the mainland would have been fully used. With limited resources, the finches would have to struggle for existence. Only the finches that were most fit would have been able to survive the several-hundred-mile journey to the islands and thrive in their new environment.

Darwin's Marriage to Emma

By the summer of 1838, Darwin felt bold enough to share his radical ideas with his father, who took them in stride. During the last several months, Darwin had struck up a close relationship with his cousin, Emma Wedgwood. However, when he brought up the subject of marrying Emma, his father warned that she came from a very strict family—Emma's family would never consider Darwin's theories as anything but heresy. Deeply in love, Darwin ignored his father's advice. He mentioned some of his notions regarding religion and nature to Emma, who was surprisingly understanding.

Darwin juggled numerous tasks, from writing books, to studying more fossils, to watching apes and orangutans at the London Zoo. As he worked, he also continued his relationship with Emma. He proposed to her on November 11, 1838. The proposal was well received by both sides of the family. Arrangements were made for Darwin to receive a handsome annual sum of money from his father. This would allow the couple to live comfortably, while Darwin continued retaining Covington's services, since research on the theory of evolution was still incomplete.

Charles and Emma were married on January 29, 1839. The couple settled into a home in London, which was already filled with scientific material. Shortly thereafter, Covington left Darwin's employment to make his own fortune. He was replaced by a man named Joseph Parslow.

The Publication of *Beagle*

During the spring of 1839, Darwin continued his research on crossbreeding. He continued to ask various experts, including farmers, questions about how they crossbred their animals. He filled page after page with his correspondences. In May, the multi-volume collection he wrote with Captain Fitzroy, *Narrative of the Surveying Voyages of HMS Adventure and Beagle*, was finally released to the public. It celebrated the *Beagle*'s voyage.

A month later, Darwin completed his N notebook, finishing his research on transmutation. Still worried about how the public would react to his developing theories, Darwin held off on publishing his findings.

In August 1839, Darwin's volume of the *Narrative* series was reissued under the title *Journal of Researches into the Geology and Natural History of the Various Countries Visited by HMS Beagle, Under the Command of Captain Fitzroy, R.N., from 1832 to 1836*. This work was better received than the previous three-volume account of the trip. The *Journal of Researches* was released in many different editions, under many different titles. The most well-known version was published in 1845, which included more details on his findings. It is this edition that remains in print today.

Shown here is the first printing of *Voyage of the Beagle*, published under the cumbersome title *Narrative of the Surveying Voyages of HMS Adventure and Beagle Between the Years 1826 and 1836 Describing Their Examination of the Southern Shores of South America and the Beagle's Circumnavigation of the Globe*. It was a composite work by Captain Fitzroy and Darwin and was the foundation for Darwin's monumental work *On the Origin of Species*. *On the Origin of Species* would become one of the most groundbreaking books in science.

NARRATIVE

OF THE

SURVEYING VOYAGES

OF HIS MAJESTY'S SHIPS

ADVENTURE AND BEAGLE,

BETWEEN

THE YEARS 1826 AND 1836,

DESCRIBING THEIR

EXAMINATION OF THE SOUTHERN SHORES

OF

SOUTH AMERICA,

AND

THE BEAGLE'S CIRCUMNAVIGATION OF THE GLOBE.

IN THREE VOLUMES.
VOL. III.

LONDON:
HENRY COLBURN, GREAT MARLBOROUGH STREET.
1839.

Researching *Origin*

By 1842, Darwin accepted his grandfather's theory that God set the universe into motion only to let species evolve on their own, combining both the creationist theory with that of evolution. During the next several months, he spent time refining the outline for his next book, which was to contain his theories. Soon thereafter, Darwin's three-year period of ill health wound down, followed almost immediately with the completion of his notes from the *Beagle* voyage.

Darwin had befriended English botanist Joseph Dalton Hooker (1817–1911) and entrusted him to examine the Tierra del Fuego plant samples. He was thrilled by Hooker's enthusiastic reception to his theories of evolution.

Soon after meeting Hooker, Darwin completed a 189-page outline on the transmutation theory. The draft proposed that animal and plant species remained unchanged until their natural environments changed. A catastrophic event, such as an earthquake, could trigger these changes in species. According to Darwin, those species that displayed these new adaptations were the ones to survive and thrive over time. Darwin hoped that this theory would explain the variation evident among species.

In September, the manuscript was 231 pages in length. Darwin finally had the confidence now to share it with Emma. Rather than calling the work heretical, she calmly accepted many of his thoughts and made constructive suggestions.

A month later, Darwin was surprised to learn that Robert Chambers's book, *Vestiges of the Natural History of Creation*, discussing transmutation, had been published. While critics bashed Chambers for ignoring Judeo-Christian beliefs surrounding the creationism theory, the book became a bestseller. Now competing against Chambers, Darwin began seeking other supporters beyond Hooker.

It was time, once again, to work on transmutation. Darwin jotted down ideas for how the process of transmutation worked. He continued to refine his theory, keenly aware that his explanation of transmutation to the scientific community and the general public needed to be as clear as possible to avoid criticism and protests of heresy.

As winter turned to spring in 1855, Darwin thought he figured out how plant life spread from place to place. After soaking seeds for several months, he then planted them. To his surprise, the seeds took root and bloomed. Darwin then began asking colleagues around the world for verification that plants could be found along the shores around the world. As the results of Darwin's queries to his colleagues came back, Darwin

Birds proved to be good specimens for the study of transmutation in progress. Darwin crossbred many variations of pigeons. By crossbreeding them himself in a controlled environment, he was able to closely examine which characteristics each generation adopted from the generation before it. Shown here is a color engraving by the artist D. Wolsenholme in 1862 of a pouter pigeon. Pouter pigeons are a clear example of how physical traits are passed from one generation to the next. Visibly different from other pigeons, the pouter pigeon has a thick upper body. Darwin went on to describe the pouter pigeon in the first chapter of *On the Origin of Species* titled "Variation Under Domestication."

was delighted to learn how far many of these plants had traveled. He also asked officials of the British survey fleet whether any crew members aboard ships had spotted animals on natural formations such as small islands and icebergs. Their account, too, confirmed Darwin's theory that species could travel from one area to another, to interbreed and create hybrid species. Darwin was delighted.

For more practical research, Darwin began breeding pigeons of different breeds. This way, he could watch the results of crossbreeding and make his own observations, instead of relying on those he made in the wild. Shortly thereafter, Charles Lyell shared with Darwin a paper titled "On the

Law Which has Regulated the Introduction of New Species," by naturalist Alfred Russel Wallace. Wallace's theories were remarkably similar to Darwin's.

Darwin was inspired. On May 14, 1856, he began writing his own essay on natural selection. Natural selection is the ability of one species to survive over another because of how well it is adapted to its environment. The intended short essay consumed the next year of his life, until exhaustion forced him to rest in the spring of 1857. He was back to work that summer, and it was clear the essay was going to become a book.

On the Origin of Species

As Darwin continued writing the essay into 1857, he saw it grow longer and longer. He became worried that no one would read such a huge volume. He also admitted to colleagues that he had been at work on the notion of man's origins for twenty years, but would not discuss it beyond fellow naturalists.

In June 1858, Wallace wrote another paper, "On the Tendency of Varieties to Depart Indefinitely from the Original Type." This time, Wallace's theories were even closer to those of Darwin's. Needless to say, Darwin was quite concerned that his own theories might not be original. He comforted himself by believing that the ideas expressed in Wallace's paper were

In the wake of the publication of *On the Origin of Species* in 1859, a great debate arose between Darwin's followers and the creationists. Opponents of Darwin used many of his theories to ridicule him, including his theory that man descended from apes. In this 1861 lithograph, Darwin is caricatured as an ape.

not identical to his. Also, as in the first paper, Darwin disagreed with several of Wallace's findings.

Weeks later, on July 1, Wallace's paper, as well as extracts from Darwin's own writings, were read at London's Linnean Society, made up of scholars who exchanged ideas in the field of biology. This was the first time Darwin's theories were presented to the public. Such revolutionary ideas as transmutation and natural selection, from not one but two naturalists, brought extreme reactions, exactly as Darwin predicted.

A few weeks afterward, Darwin took his family on vacation. He spent time trying to find ways to shorten his manuscript, which he finally shared with Hooker in March 1859. In the months that followed, Darwin fell ill again, but he managed to proofread the manuscript. He sent the completed text to John Murray Publishers in October. He then took his family to Yorkshire, where he sought treatment for his illness. This allowed him to stay away from London and the reaction the book's publication was sure to elicit.

Darwin received a finished copy of the book, *On the Origin of Species by Means of Natural Selection, Or the Preservation of Favored Races in the Struggle for Life* in November 1859. Finally, after more than twenty years, Darwin had completed his research, tested his theories, and presented them to the world. It was sure to create much controversy.

CHAPTER 5

In November 1859, *On the Origin of Species* went on sale. It caused an immediate sensation. The 1,250 copies available sold out quickly. Darwin started making changes for the demanded second edition. He completed those changes in early December, and John Murray more than doubled the print run to 3,000 copies. A German translation was also under way, which would bring Darwin's theories to other parts of Europe.

EVOLUTION OF THE SPECIES

In the *Origin of Species*, Darwin explained the theories of natural selection and transmutation, along with many others involved in the process of evolution. Natural selection is the theory that living organisms adapt to their changing environments in order to survive. The organisms that adapt the best to their environments are the most "fit," or best suited to their environments. They therefore have the best chances for survival. Organisms that don't adapt well to their environments eventually die off, unable to pass on their traits.

Darwin believed that variation among living organisms in the wild was a result of adaptations to new environments. For example, scientists today believe that a meteor struck the

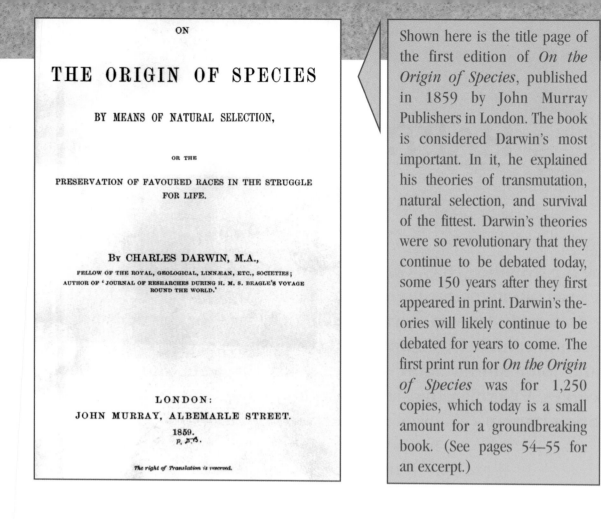

ON

THE ORIGIN OF SPECIES

BY MEANS OF NATURAL SELECTION,

OR THE

PRESERVATION OF FAVOURED RACES IN THE STRUGGLE
FOR LIFE.

BY CHARLES DARWIN, M.A.,
FELLOW OF THE ROYAL, GEOLOGICAL, LINNÆAN, ETC., SOCIETIES;
AUTHOR OF 'JOURNAL OF RESEARCHES DURING H. M. S. BEAGLE'S VOYAGE
ROUND THE WORLD.'

LONDON:
JOHN MURRAY, ALBEMARLE STREET.
1859.

The right of Translation is reserved.

Shown here is the title page of the first edition of *On the Origin of Species*, published in 1859 by John Murray Publishers in London. The book is considered Darwin's most important. In it, he explained his theories of transmutation, natural selection, and survival of the fittest. Darwin's theories were so revolutionary that they continue to be debated today, some 150 years after they first appeared in print. Darwin's theories will likely continue to be debated for years to come. The first print run for *On the Origin of Species* was for 1,250 copies, which today is a small amount for a groundbreaking book. (See pages 54–55 for an excerpt.)

earth during the reign of the dinosaurs 144 million years ago. The meteor filled the atmosphere with dust and dirt, which blocked the sun for years. This change in the environment was such that the dinosaurs could not adapt to it, causing them to eventually die out. Other species that were smaller required less food and water to live. As a result, they reproduced and passed on their traits to their offspring, multiplying and thriving. They were more fit to survive.

Darwin wrote in the *Origin of Species*, "Natural selection acts only by taking advantage of slight successive variations; she can never take a great and sudden leap, but must advance by short and sure, though slow, steps." Darwin referred to this gradual change as transmutation. Mutations are differences between individual organisms in a species. One creature might be a little stronger or faster than the others, making it more able to fight off possible attackers. Thus, it is more fit to survive. Transmutation is the gradual change in physical differences over time.

Darwin filled many notebooks with his observations of how these mutations occurred in nature. The changes that allow the creature or plant to survive are passed along to the next generation. They then become a natural part of the species's makeup. Those traits allow the organism to survive in its environment. This ability to survive is called natural selection. Natural selection is also summarized in the phrase survival of the fittest. √

Public Opinion

The public began debating Darwin's ideas in the pages of local newspapers and down at the local taverns. Many people could not quite follow Darwin's writing and were confused by the forces behind natural selection. Several people tried to fit them into their own religious views.

In the scientific community, people had opposing viewpoints. Friends of Darwin, such as Thomas Henry Huxley and Hooker, defended his work. Huxley even coined the term "Darwinism" to describe Darwin's theories. Huxley called himself "Darwin's bulldog" as he viciously defended Darwin's reasoning because the author himself was too ill to do it. Meanwhile, critic Richard Owen attacked Darwinism as being a danger to society because of its lack of religious values. Within six months, talk of natural selection had spread around the world, prompting vigorous debate.

The Debate

On June 30, 1860, New York University professor of chemistry John William Draper spoke at the British Association for the Advancement of Science. The subject of Draper's speech was Darwin's theories as they influenced social progress. The argument was that evolution gave humans a better sense of their place in the world than religion. Bishop Samuel Wilberforce and Huxley were also present. Wilberforce attacked Darwin's theories for going against religious beliefs. Huxley supported Darwin. The encounter came to be know as the Wilberforce-Huxley debate.

Surprisingly, Captain Fitzroy of the *Beagle* was also in attendance. Fitzroy raised the Bible and asked people to follow its teachings and not Darwin's theory. The debate lasted for four hours. Although Darwin caused so much debate, he was too ill to attend.

Six months later, in January 1861, Huxley purchased the publication the *Natural History Review*, using it as a forum to promote Darwin's views on evolution and natural selection. In his very first issue, Huxley wrote about the physical similarities between humans and apes, something he theorized, like Darwin, years earlier. Huxley sent a complimentary copy to his rival Bishop Wilberforce and then set out to engage Owen in debate over the next few months. The public could not get enough of the sophisticated battle.

Darwin's Next Book

Within the year of *Origin*'s publication, it remained a strong seller in England with translations in German, Dutch, and French. While vacationing with his daughter Henrietta, Darwin's

The debate of evolution was an extremely hot topic upon the publication of *On the Origin of Species*. People who stood on each side of the debate went to great lengths to outwit their opponents. This parody, showing a stern-looking Bishop Wiberforce, was published as "The Bishop of Oxford" in the July 24, 1869, issue of *Vanity Fair* magazine. Wilberforce was a vocal protester of Darwin's theory of evolution. His position on evolution was that it went against the Judeo-Christian teachings of the Bible. On June 30, 1860, he engaged in the historic debate with John William Draper and Thomas Henry Huxley at the British Association for the Advancement of Science, attacking Darwin's theories.

attention was captured by the way certain insects pollinated only certain species of flower. As his research on breeding pigeons was complete, he turned to study orchids. Once people learned of his latest interest, they sent Darwin orchid samples. The house was full of specimens once again. Darwin wrote a book on the subject titled, *On the Various Contrivances by Which British and Foreign Orchids Are Fertilized by Insects*. It was published in May 1862.

Darwin concentrated on orchids, while battling his recurring illness. Huxley began to travel the country to promote Darwin's work. In 1863, Huxley's own *Man's Place in Nature* was published.

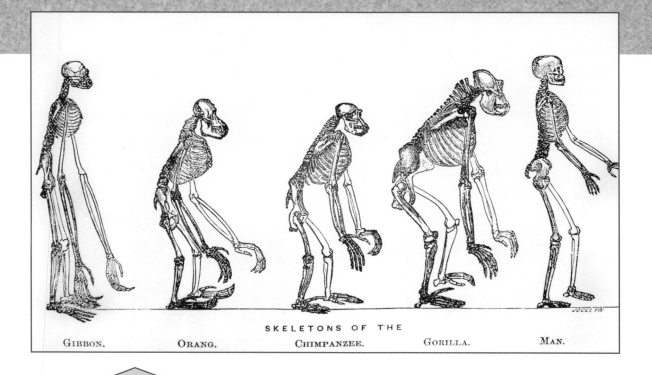

SKELETONS OF THE

GIBBON.   ORANG.   CHIMPANZEE.   GORILLA.   MAN.

Known as "Darwin's bulldog" for the ferocity with which he defended Darwin's ideas, Thomas Henry Huxley created this drawing in 1863 of his view of the evolution of man. Following Darwin's theory that man descended from the ape, Huxley's drawing, titled "Evidence as to Man's Place in Nature," shows the evolutionary history of human beings. According to Huxley, our first descendant was the gibbon, an ape that currently inhabits southeastern Asia. Following the gibbon is the orang, a shortened name for another type of ape called an orangutan. Following that are the chimpanzee, gorilla, and man.

Huxley's book furthered evolutionary ideas by including his theory that man descended from apes.

As expected, the church officials took a negative view of these new theories that rocked the foundations of their religious beliefs. So did Owen, who accidentally furthered Darwin's cause in 1863 when he convinced the British Museum to purchase a fossil. This particular fossil was a hybrid between lizard and bird called archaeopteryx. Discovered in the Jurassic Solnhofen Limestone of southern Germany, the fossil is considered by many paleontologists—scientists who study fossils—to be the first bird species that descended from the line of reptiles, dating back 150 million years. Paleontologists view archaeopteryx as a species that was in the transitional stage between reptile and bird. In Darwin's eyes, this fossil was a perfect example of transmutation in process.

The Debate Continues

Debate over the concept of evolution did not slow down. With the church marshalling its forces to condemn evolution, the X Club was founded. The X Club was made up of like-minded scientists who discussed current scientific theory without fear of interruption by the church. The club began publishing *Nature* magazine as an outlet to share its views with the general public. The magazine remains in print today.

Controversy continued over evolution as a frail Darwin made a rare appearance in November 1864 to accept the Copley Medal, the highest award from the Royal Society of London. Certain factions within the Royal Society wanted to present the medal to Adam Sedgwick, Darwin's geology professor from Cambridge. But the medal was awarded to Darwin under the condition that *Origin* not be named as a factor in the decision.

Queen Victoria remained above the arguments, choosing not to get involved and never recognizing Darwin's contributions. Several of Britain's prime ministers, including Benjamin Disraeli, however, did not agree with Darwin's theories. In fact, when asked where he stood on the subject of where man came from, heaven or ape, Disraeli replied that he was on the side of the angels.

Darwin remained quite ill during this period, not returning to London and the society until April 1866. A year later, he began working on a book specifically about human origins. The work grew too large for one book, so he divided it into two volumes: *Descent of Man* (1871) and *Selection in Relation to Sex* (1871). He also returned to writing about other life-forms in *The Variation of Animals and Plants under Domestication* (1868).

Between projects and illnesses, Darwin continued to refine his work. A decade after its first publication, the fifth edition of *Origin* was released. The sixth edition, published in 1871, used the word evolution for the first time. With *Descent* a huge success as well, Darwin divided his time between revising the two works. In April 1874, he completed work on *Descent*'s second edition. This was the last time Darwin wrote about evolution.

Darwin continued to write, but his topics ranged from musings on plant life to a biography of his grandfather, as well as his own autobiography, *The Autobiography of Charles Darwin 1809–1882*. Along the way, he complained to Emma of being bored, of not being challenged further. His health, never good since he first set out for sea, continued to deteriorate. Finally, on April 19, 1882, Darwin died. He was buried at Westminster Abbey, some 20 feet (6 m) from another revolutionary English scientist: Isaac Newton.

CHAPTER 6

Darwin was by no means the only person who supported the theory of evolution. However, Darwin was the only person to create a body of work on the subject, earning respect as both a naturalist and a geologist. He gained supporters and went public with his theories. Darwin's theories were not presented just to fellow scientists. They were released in book form that anyone, not just scholars or the rich, could buy. As Darwin was well established and respected, and the first person to do intense research on evolution, he became the authority.

THE EVOLUTION OF DARWINISM

Ever since *Origin* was first published in 1859, people have debated its findings. Many cannot accept the idea that man evolved from other life-forms. Their religion tells them differently. Others find it difficult to grasp the concepts without physical evidence—seeing is believing.

The Scopes Trial

The simmering debate in the United States finally exploded in a celebrated 1925 court case in Dayton, Tennessee. High school science teacher John T. Scopes was arrested and tried for violating the state's antievolution statute. The statute prohibited the

This photograph of high school science teacher John T. Scopes was taken on June 16, 1925, less than one month before the monumental Scopes trial began on July 10. Scopes became the poster boy for the debate over teaching evolution in public schools after he was arrested for violating Tennessee's antievolution statute. Quickly named "the Monkey Trial" after the theory that man descended from apes, the case attracted nearly 5,000 spectators to the tiny Rhea County Court House. The Monkey Trial set a new precedent for the evolution debate. In the following decades, numerous legal battles would take place over evolution and its constitutionality. John T. Scopes and the Monkey Trial were pivotal to the ongoing debate over evolution.

teaching of evolution in public schools. In the forthcoming trial, the constitutionality of the antievolution law was going to be decided. The U.S. Constitution states that there must be a separation between church and state. This means that religious views should not be presented in the classroom or any other government-sponsored building. The antievolution statute, which banned the teaching of evolution but supported creationism, was argued to be in violation of the Constitution. Nearly every newspaper in the nation and most around the world covered the story. Darwin's theory was big news once again.

Prosecuting the case was William Jennings Bryan, a former politician. Although Bryan had not practiced law in thirty years,

William Jennings Bryan was a strong supporter of banning the teaching of evolution in public schools. He so strongly believed in his cause that he offered to take on the case of the prosecution in the Scopes trial even though he had not practiced law in more than thirty years. Bryan is shown here with arms outstretched at the trial in this photograph taken on July 19, 1925. Bryan ultimately won the case over his opponent, Clarence Darrow.

he volunteered his services as prosecutor because he was a strong supporter of banning the teaching of evolution. Previously, he led the fight to ban the teaching of evolution by helping fifteen states, including Tennessee, adopt laws against it.

Famed attorney Clarence Darrow headed the defense. Darrow, a strong leader against capital punishment, had defended hundreds of people. He had spent years defending the underdog. Darrow was ready to take on Bryan.

The trial, which began on July 10, 1925, was a media circus. The tiny Rhea County Court House, presided over by Judge John

T. Raulston, was stuffed with spectators, journalists, and radio broadcasters. Despite both sides of the case being flush with lawyers, Darrow and Bryan were the main speakers. More and more people arrived to watch as the trial continued. Nearly 5,000 people came to watch the historic proceedings each day. Given the popularity of Darwin's theories, including the proposition that man descended from apes, the case was quickly dubbed the Monkey Trial.

One of the most memorable arguments of the trial occurred when Bryan was called to the witness stand to testify as an expert on the Bible. Darrow managed to get Bryan to concede that not everything written in the Bible should be taken literally. This was a huge admission given the tenor of the trial.

Ultimately, Darrow lost the case, and the antievolution law was upheld. Scopes was fined $100 for teaching evolution. It was not until 1968—forty-three years after the Scopes trial—that the U.S. Supreme Court fully outlawed banning the teaching of evolution in the case of *Epperson v. Arkansas*.

Evolution to Date

Ever since the Scopes trial, countries around the world have struggled with how best to teach scientific theory without treating religious texts as nothing more than modern mythology. The struggle also continues in the United States. Schools around the country have battled over how to present the theory of evolution as well as the biblical version of creation, which today is called creation science. Many school districts have argued to teach both creationism and evolution side by side. But this proposal has ignited a different debate, that over the role of religion in public schools and the separation of church and state.

Tribune EDITION

25 ★ ★ ★ ★

TWO CENTS | THREE CENTS | FOUR CENTS
In Greater New York | Within 200 Miles | Elsewhere

Note rley, View

h Aim s Occu- Seeks League

sult Reply

givings d Sees Offing

len une's Berlin ribune Inc. any's reply note, which imultaneous s, and Lon- ted in both circles here Germany's d viewpoint ry into the

y along the ld Tribune on of Allied nost certain nference of ntatives for erlin is not

Scopes Guilty, $100 Fine; Defies the Law as Unfair; Darrow Rushes Appeal

British Wireless 'Phone "Calls Up" U. S. Warship, 8,000 Miles Away

From the Herald Tribune's London Bureau
Copyright, 1925, New York Tribune Inc.

LONDON, July 21.—Gerald Marcuse, an amateur radio operator, of Caterham, Surrey, talked on the telephone wireless to the radio operator of the United States cruiser Seattle, 600 miles east of Australia, for twenty minutes this morning. This is believed to establish a record for wireless telephony with an amateur set. Marcuse used a low wave of 45 meters. This morning he got in touch through code with Lieutenant Schnell on the Seattle. The signals came through so strong that Marcuse suggested they try telephony, with highly satisfactory results.

From the New York Herald Tribune's Washington Bureau

WASHINGTON, July 21.—Radio experts here to-night declared that the conversation between an amateur wireless operator in England and the cruiser Seattle off Australia establishes a record for telephony on short wave lengths. The Seattle was about 8,000 miles air line from England. "It is a remarkable feat," said W. E. Downey, radio expert of the Department of Commerce.

The British Marconi Company's beam station in England had conversed by telephone with Australians, but used an extremely high power commercial set.

Coolidge Hits 'Overhead' in

Dayton Breeds Whale of Issue

Evolution Trial, Marked by Bitterness, Ends in 'Love Feast' After Teacher Flays Tennessee Act

Verdict Ordered, Found in 5 Minutes

Only Bryan-Darrow Animosity Remains, Commoner Putting 9 Bible Questions to Opponent

By Forrest Davis
A Staff Correspondent

DAYTON, Tenn., July 21.—In the abrupt end of the Tennessee evolution trial this morning John Thomas Scopes emerged as a full length figure. Hitherto dwarfed in the mighty legal battle, he to-day declared the faith that is in him in ringing terms.

Young Scopes, convicted of teaching evolution against the laws of Tennessee, stood before the bar of

---

This newspaper headline shows the importance of the Scopes trial and the amount of media coverage it received. Though the trial took place in rural Dayton, Tennessee, this Wednesday, July 22, 1925, issue of the *New York Tribune* used the trial verdict as its top story. The story went on to explain that John T. Scopes was found guilty of violating the Tennessee law prohibiting the teaching of evolution in the state's public schools. (See page 55 for an excerpt.)

This 1881 portrait shows Charles Darwin about a year before he died in 1882. By this time, *On the Origin of Species* was in its sixth edition. Darwin had won the Copley Medal from the Royal Society of London. He had published *Descent of Man*, which soon went into a second edition, and *Selection in Relation to Sex*. He continued to write other books on a range of topics, and by the end of his life, wrote a biography of his grandfather as well as his own autobiography chronicling his monumental life. Charles Darwin is considered one of the greatest scientists, and his theory of evolution one of the greatest breakthroughs. Darwin's ideas were so influential that they continue to be debated today.

In 1999, the state of Kansas dropped evolution from the state's public school curriculum, bowing to pressure from religious groups. But then in 2001, the decision was reversed, once again adding the theory of evolution to the state curriculum.

A different but related dispute broke out at Grand Canyon National Park in Arizona. In 2003, three plaques that quoted the Bible on how the world was created in six days were removed. The U.S. National Park Service insisted that the plaques be returned out of respect for differing points of view.

Then in February 2004, Georgia's school superintendent Kathy Cox suggested removing the word "evolution" from the school curriculum. She suggested using the phrase "biological changes over time" to replace it. This would teach the ideas, she argued, without the word "evolution" acting as a trigger for debate. A public outcry forced the proposal off the table.

In March 2004, the Ohio school board heard six hours of testimony and voted thirteen to five in favor of adding the religious theory of creation to the school lesson plan. The course, "Critical Analysis of Evolution," was intended to be an optional set of lessons aimed at a new statewide science curriculum. Scientific groups criticized the move, and parents were contemplating a lawsuit. As you can see from these recent debates, the battle over evolutionary theory is not going to end anytime soon.

TIMELINE

1809	—	Darwin is born in Shrewsbury, England, on February 12.
1831	—	Darwin graduates from Christ's College, Cambridge, on April 26.
1831	—	Darwin leaves England aboard the HMS *Beagle* on December 27.
1835	—	The *Beagle* reaches Galápagos Islands on September 15.
1836	—	Darwin returns to England after a five-year voyage on the *Beagle* on October 2.
1859	—	*On the Origin of Species by Means of Natural Selection* is published in November.
1860	—	*Origin* goes into its second printing of 3,000 copies on January 7.
1860	—	Thomas Henry Huxley and Bishop Samuel Wilberforce debate Darwin's theory of evolution on June 30.
1862	—	*On the Various Contrivances by Which British and Foreign Orchids Are Fertilized by Insects* is published in May.
1868	—	*The Variation of Animals and Plants Under Domestication* is published.

1871	— *Descent of Man* and *Selection in Relation to Sex* are published. Darwin uses the word "evolution" for the first time in his sixth edition of *Origin*.
1879	— Darwin publishes a biography of his grandfather, titled *Life of Erasmus Darwin*, on November 19.
1882	— Darwin dies on April 19.
1925	— The Scopes trial begins in Dayton, Tennessee, on July 10.
1968	— In *Epperson v. Arkansas*, the Supreme Court finds that the Arkansas law prohibiting the teaching of evolution is unconstitutional.
1999	— The state of Kansas drops evolution from the state's public school curriculum.
2001	— The state of Kansas reverses the 1999 decision and adds the theory of evolution to the state curriculum.
2004	— The Ohio school board votes thirteen to five in favor of adding the religious theory of creation to the school curriculum.

PRIMARY SOURCE TRANSCRIPTIONS

Page 15: From *Zoonomia; or, The Laws of Organic Life*

All animals have a similar origin, viz. from a single living filament; and that the difference of their forms and qualities has arisen only from the different irritabilities and sensibilities, or voluntarities, or associabilities, of this original living filament; and perhaps in some degree from the different forms of the particles of the fluids, by which it has been first stimulated into activity. And that from hence, as Linnæus has conjectured in respect to the vegetable world, it is not impossible, but the great variety of species of animals, which now tenant the earth, may have had their origin from the mixture of a few natural orders. And that those animal and vegetable mules, which could continue their species, have done so, and constitute the numerous families of animals and vegetables which now exist; and that those mules, which were produced with imperfect organs of generation, perished without reproduction, according to the observation of Aristotle; and are the animals, which we now call mules.

Pages 19 and 31: From *The Journal of a Voyage in HMS Beagle*

The natural history of these islands is eminently curious, and well deserves attention. Most of the organic productions are aboriginal creations, found nowhere else; there is even a difference between the inhabitants of the different islands; yet all show a marked relationship with those of America, though separated from that continent by an open space of ocean, between 500 and 600 miles in width. The archipelago is a little world within itself, or rather a satellite attached to America, whence it has derived a few stray colonists, and has received the general character of its indigenous productions. Considering the small size of the islands, we feel the more astonished at the number of their aboriginal beings, and at their confined range. Seeing every height crowned with its crater, and the boundaries of most of the lava- streams still distinct, we are led to believe that within a period geologically recent the unbroken ocean was here spread out. Hence, both in space and time, we seem to be brought somewhat near to that great fact—that mystery of mysteries—the first appearance of new beings on this earth.

Page 27: From *First Notebook on Transmutation of Species*

In July opened the first notebook on *Transmutation of Species*. Had been greatly struck from about the previous March on character of South American fossils and species on Galápagos Archipelago. These facts (especially the latter) origin all my views.

Page 38: From *On the Origin of Species*

In order to make it clear how, as I believe, natural selection acts, I must beg permission to give one or two imaginary illustrations. Let us take the case of a wolf, which preys on various animals, securing some by craft, some by strength, and some by fleetness; and let us suppose that the fleetest prey, a deer for instance, had from any change in the country increased in numbers, or that other prey had decreased in numbers, during that season of the year when the wolf is hardest pressed for food. I can under such circumstances see no reason to doubt that the swiftest and slimmest wolves would have the best chance of surviving, and so be preserved or selected—provided always that they retained strength to master their prey at this or at some other period of the year, when they might be compelled to prey on other animals . . . Let us now take a more complex case. Certain plants excrete a sweet juice, apparently for the sake of eliminating something injurious from their sap: this is effected by glands at the base of the stipules in some Leguminosae, and at the back of the leaf of the common laurel. This juice, though small in quantity, is greedily sought by insects. Let us now suppose a little sweet juice or nectar to be excreted by the inner bases of the petals of a flower. In this case insects in seeking the nectar would get dusted with pollen, and would certainly often transport the pollen from one flower to the stigma of another flower. The flowers of two distinct individuals of the same species would thus get crossed; and the act of crossing, we have good reason to believe (as will hereafter be more fully alluded to), would produce very vigorous seedlings, which consequently would have the best chance of flourishing and surviving.

Some of these seedlings would probably inherit the nectar-excreting power. Those in individual flowers which had the largest glands or nectaries, and which excreted most nectar, would be oftenest visited by insects, and would be oftenest crossed; and so in the long-run would gain the upper hand.

Page 49: From the *New York Tribune*

DAYTON, Tenn., July 21.—In the abrupt end of the Tennessee evolution trial this morning John Thomas Scopes emerged as a full length figure. Hithero dwarfed in the mighty legal battle, he to-day declared the faith that is in him in ringing terms.

Young Scopes, convicted of teaching evolution against the laws of Tennessee, stood before the bar of justice awaiting sentence. He leaned his tanned student's face toward Judge John L. Raulston. Arms bared to the elbows, where a yellow shirt appeared, were folded behind his back. Judge Raulston, fiery Fundamentalist, was kindly. Through confusion he omitted to ask scopes if he wished to make a statement before sentencing. He imposed the minimum fine, $100. Then the guilty pedagogue, John R. Neal having interrupted, spoke.

Calls Statute Unjust

"Your honor," he said earnestly, the eyes of the courtroom fixed on him for the first time since his extraordinary trial opened, "I feel that I have been convicted of an unjust statute."

"I will continue in the future, as I have in the past, to oppose this law in any way I can. Any other action would be in violation of my ideals of academic freedom—that is, to teach the truth, as guaranteed in our constitution, of personal and religious freedom. I think the fine is unjust."

For the moment Darrow, implacable foe of religious intolerance; Bryan, crusader fore the literal bible; Malone, gifted orator, and the other spangled champions of the divided forces, were forgotten. It dawned upon the courtroom that Scopes, willing victim of the "steel door" law, had made a stand for his convictions, and that, despite the differences of opinions to his moral guilt, he stood convicted of a misdemeanor.

GLOSSARY

botany The branch of biology that deals with plant life.

coral A group of organisms that produces a hard outer skeleton. Coral deposits often accumulate to form reefs or islands in warm seas.

creationism The belief in the literal interpretation of the Bible's account of the creation of the universe.

crossbreeding The mating of individuals of different breeds, varieties, or species to produce a new form of life.

entomologist A person who studies insects.

environment The habitat in which particular species live and to which they adapt.

finch A songbird having a short, stout bill.

fossil A remnant of an organism, such as a skeleton or leaf imprint, embedded and preserved in the earth's crust.

geology The scientific study of the origin, history, and structure of the earth.

hybrid A mixed species formed by the breeding of two or more different species.

hybridization The process of interbreeding two different species.

natural selection The process by which a species survives and reproduces because of how well adapted to its environment it is.

naturalist A person who believes that scientific theories and laws explain the workings of the universe.

ornithology The branch of zoology that deals with the study of birds.

species An organism belonging to a group with similar biological traits.

survival of the fittest A phrase used to describe species that are most likely to survive because of how well adapted they are to their environment.

taxidermy The practice of stuffing and mounting the skins of animals.

theory A principle designed to explain occurrences that are often repeated in nature.

transmutation Gradual change in physical differences of species over time.

zoology The branch of biology that deals with animals and animal life, including the study of the structure, physiology, development, and classification of animals.

OR MORE INFORMATION

Charles Darwin Foundation, Inc.
407 N. Washington St., Ste. 105
Falls Church, VA 22046
Web site: http://www.galapagos.org
(703) 538-6833
e-mail: darwin@galapagos.org

Charles Darwin Foundation for the Galápagos Islands
Av. 6 de Diciembre N 36-109 y Pasaje California
Post Box 17-01-3891
Quito, Ecuador
Web site: http://www.darwinfoundation.org

Galápagos Conservation Trust
5 Derby Street
London, W1J 7AB, UK
44 (0) 20 7629 5049
e-mail: gct@gct.org
Web site: http://www.gct.org

Web Sites

Due to the changing nature of Internet links, the Rosen Publishing Group, Inc. has developed an online list of Web sites related to the subject of this book. This site is updated regularly. Please use this link to access the list:

www.rosenlinks.com/psrsdt/date

FOR FURTHER READING

Browne, E. Janet. *Charles Darwin: The Power of Place.* Princeton, NJ: Princeton University Press, 2003.

Keynes, Randal. *Darwin, His Daughter and Human Evolution.* New York: Riverhead Books, 2002.

Keynes, Richard. *Darwin. Fossils, Finches, and Fuegians: Charles Darwin's Adventures and Discoveries on the Beagle, 1832-1836.* London: HarperCollins, 2002.

Ruse, Michael. *Darwin and Design: Does Evolution Have a Purpose?* Cambridge, MA: Harvard University Press, 2003.

Stott, Rebecca. *Darwin and the Barnacle: The Story of One Tiny Creature and History's Most Spectacular Scientific Breakthrough.* New York: W.W. Norton & Co., 2003.

BIBLIOGRAPHY

AboutDarwin.com. Retrieved January 2004 (http://www.aboutdarwin.com).

Bowler, Peter J. *Evolution: The History of an Idea*. Berkeley, CA: University of California Press, 2003.

"Charles Darwin: British Naturalist." Retrieved January 2004 (http://www2.lucidcafe.com/lucidcafe/library/96feb/darwin.html).

Darwin, Charles. *The Autobiography of Charles Darwin 1809–1882*. New York: W. W. Norton & Co., 1993.

Darwin's Theory of Evolution. Retrieved January 2004 (http://www.darwins-theory-of-evolution.com).

Dawkins, Richard. *River Out of Eden: A Darwinian View of Life*. New York: Basic Books, 1995.

Eldredge, Niles. *Reinventing Darwin: The Great Debate at the High Table of Evolutionary Theory*. New York: John Wiley & Sons, 1995.

Indiana University of Pennsylvania. "Darwin's Theory of Evolution." Retrieved January 2004 (http://nsm1.nsm.iup.edu/rwinstea/darwin.shtm).

Keynes, Richard Darwin. *Fossils, Finches, and Fuegians: Charles Darwin's Adventures and Discoveries on the Beagle, 1832–1836*. London: Harper Collins, 2002.

Online Literature Library. "Charles Darwin." Retrieved January 2004 (http://www.literature.org/authors/darwin-charles).

SpaceandMotion.com. "Charles Darwin: The Theory of Evolution." Retrieved January 2004 (http://www.spaceandmotion.com/Charles-Darwin-Theory-Evolution.htm).

TalkOrigins.org. "Evolution FAQs." Retrieved January 2004 (http://www.talkorigins.org/origins/faqs-evolution.html).

PRIMARY SOURCE IMAGE LIST

Title Page: Watercolor by Owen Stanley of the HMS *Beagle* in Sydney Harbor, 1841. Housed in the National Maritime Museum in London, England.

Page 5: Photograph of Charles Darwin's sextant from his voyage on the HMS *Beagle*. Housed in the Royal Geographical Society in London, England.

Page 9: Engraving of deck plans of the HMS *Beagle,* titled *HMS Beagle, Middle Section Fore and Aft,* from 1832.

Page 12: *The Harkort Factory at Burg Wetter* by Alfred Rethel, oil on canvas, 1834.

Page 15: *Zoonomia; or, The Laws of Organic Life, vol. II* by Erasmus Darwin, 1796.

Page 17: Watercolor of the HMS *Beagle* by Conrad Martens titled *Mt. Sarmiento 6800.* 1834.

Page 19: Manuscript of Darwin's account on the HMS *Beagle* titled *The Journal of a Voyage in H.M.S.* Beagle, *1831–1836,* housed in the Royal College of Surgeons in London, England.

Page 23. Photograph of microscope used by Charles Darwin, taken in 1959.

Page 25. Illustration by Charles Darwin in 1845, published in the *Journal of Researches into the Geology and Natural History of the Various Countries Visited by HMS* Beagle, *Under the Command of Captain FitzRoy, R.N., from 1832 to 1836.*

Page 27: Drawing by Charles Darwin in 1837, in his *First Notebook on Transmutation of Species.*

Page 31: Title page of *Narrative of the Surveying Voyages of HMS Adventure and Beagle,* by Charles Darwin, published in 1839.

Page 33: Color engraving titled *Portrait of a Pouter Pigeon* by D. Wolsenholme, 1862.

Page 35: Color lithograph of "This is the ape of form," 1861.

Page 38: Title page of *On the Origin of Species by Means of Natural Selection*, by Charles Darwin, Published by John Murray, 1859.

Page 41: Color engraving of "The Bishop of Oxford" by Ape. Published in *Vanity Fair* in 1869.

Page 42: Engraving of "Evidence as to Man's Place in Nature" by Thomas Henry Huxley, 1863.

Page 46: Photograph of John Scopes, taken on June 16, 1925.

Page 47: William Jennings Bryan in court, photographed on July 19, 1925.

Page 49: Newspaper article "Scopes Guilty, $100 Fine; Defies the Law as Unfair; Darrow Rushes Appeal" by Forrest Davis. Published on July 22, 1925, in the *New York Herald.*

Page 50: Photograph of Charles Darwin by Julia Margaret Cameron, 1881.

INDEX

B

Bonnet, Charles, 13
Bryan, William Jennings, 46–47, 48
Buffon, Georges, 13–14

C

Chambers, Robert, 32
Covington, Syms, 20, 24, 30
creationism, explanation of, 11
creation science, 48
crossbreeding, 28, 30, 33

D

Darrow, Clarence, 47, 48
Darwin, Charles
    childhood and education of, 6–10
    death of, 44
    marriage of, 29–30
    research and publications by, 24–36,
        37–39, 40–41, 44
    voyage aboard the *Beagle*, 16–23
    and winning of Copley Medal, 43
Darwin, Erasmus (brother), 6, 7
Darwin, Erasmus (grandfather), 6, 14, 31, 44
Darwin, Robert (father), 6–7, 8, 14, 20, 29
Darwin, Susannah (mother), 6
degeneration, 13
Descent of Man, 44
Disraeli, Benjamin, 43
Draper, John William, 40

E

Edmonstone, John, 7
Epperson v. Arkansas, 48

evolution, theory of

    controversy and debate over, 39, 40,
        43, 45
    and education, 45–51
    explanation of, 8
    history of, 13–14

F

Fitzroy, Robert, 14, 15, 16, 18, 20, 26–27,
    30, 40

G

Grant, Robert, 8

H

Henslow, Reverend John Stevens, 8, 10,
    17, 19, 20
Hooker, Joseph Dalton, 31, 32, 36, 39
Hope, Reverend Frederick, 9
Huxley, Thomas Henry, 39, 40, 41–42
hybridization, 13

J

*Journal of Researches/Voyage of the
    Beagle*, 27, 30

L

Lamarck, Jean-Baptiste, 8
Linnaeus, Carolus, 13
Linnean Society, 34
Lyell, Charles, 21, 33

M

mutations, 38–39

N

Narrative of the Surveying Voyages of HMS Adventure and Beagle, 30
natural selection, 34, 36, 37, 39, 40
Nature magazine, 43

O

On the Origin of Species, 36, 37, 38, 40, 43, 44, 45
Owen, Fanny, 8, 10
Owen, Richard, 39, 40, 42

P

Parslow, Joseph, 30
Peacock, Reverend George, 10
Plinian Society, 7

R

Ramsay, Marmaduke, 10
Royal Geological Society, 24

S

Scopes, John T., 45, 48
Scopes Monkey Trial, 45–48
Sebright, Sir John, 28–29
Sedgwick, Adam, 10, 43

T

transmutation, 27, 28, 30, 31, 32, 36, 37, 38, 39, 43

W

Wallace, Alfred Russel, 34–36
Wedgwood, Emma, 29, 30, 32, 44
Wedgwood, Josiah, 6
Wilberforce, Bishop Samuel, 40

X

X Club, 43

Z

Zoonomia, 14

Photo Credits

About the Author

Robert Greenberger is a senior editor at DC Comics, and is also a freelance writer. He has written numerous *Star Trek* novels in addition to a wide range of nonfiction for young adults. He makes his home in Connecticut with his wife, Deb, and children, Kate and Robbie.

Editor: Nicholas Croce; Photo Researcher: Jeffrey Wendt